LIFE SCIENCE PROJECTS for kids

A PROJECT GUIDE TO MAMMALS

Christine Petersen

Mitchell Lane

PUBLISHERS

P.O. Box 196
Hockessin, Delaware 19707
Visit us on the web: www.mitchelllane.com
Comments? email us: mitchelllane@mitchelllane.com

A Project Guide to:
Exploring Earth's Biomes • Fish and Amphibians •
Mammals • Projects in Genetics • Reptiles and Birds •
Sponges, Worms, and Mollusks

Copyright © 2011 by Mitchell Lane Publishers

All rights reserved. No part of this book
may be reproduced without written permission
from the publisher. Printed and bound in the
United States of America.

PUBLISHER'S NOTE: The facts on which the story
in this book is based have been thoroughly
researched. Documentation of such research
can be found on page 44. While every possible
effort has been made to ensure accuracy, the
publisher will not assume liability for damages
caused by inaccuracies in the data, and
makes no warranty on the accuracy of the
information contained herein.

To reflect current usage, we have chosen to
use the secular era designations BCE
("before the common era") and CE ("of the
common era") instead of the traditional
designations BC ("before Christ") and AD
(*anno Domini*, "in the year of the Lord").

Library of Congress
Cataloging-in-Publication Data

Petersen, Christine.
  A project guide to mammals / Christine
Petersen.
      p. cm. — (Life science projects for kids)
  Includes bibliographical references and
index.
  ISBN 978-1-58415-875-2 (library bound)
  1. Mammals—Juvenile literature. 2. Science
projects—Juvenile literature. I. Title.
  QL706.2.P48 2011
  599.078—dc22
                                              2010008954

Printing   1   2   3   4   5   6   7   8   9

                                              PLB

CONTENTS

Introduction...4

Classification 7

Watching Wildlife 11

Tracks 15

Snowshoes 19

Baffling!...23

In a Pack 26

Build a Bat Box.......................................29

Population Census 35

Bones 38

Respiration 41

Further Reading 44

    Books 44

    Works Consulted...........................44

    On the Internet.............................45

Glossary..46

Index..47

INTRODUCTION

Earth is home to an amazing diversity of life. Scientists have already identified approximately 1.75 million species. These can be found in Earth's coldest and warmest environments, in deserts and in lush rain forests. Life thrives even in the deepest oceans, in soils, and high in the atmosphere. One-quarter of these are plants, ranging in complexity from the simplest algae to huge redwood trees. Most animal species are invertebrates—animals without backbones—such as insects, worms, snails, and corals. Animals with backbones are called vertebrates. This group includes fish, amphibians, reptiles, birds, and mammals.

It's easy for humans to feel separate from nature. Many of us do not live in wild places, and we may not spend a great deal of time outdoors. But a quick self-examination will confirm that you (and all humans) are an animal that fits into one of these groups. Your backbone makes you a vertebrate. Touch the top of your head. Chances are, it's covered in a layer of hair. Hair is a characteristic found only among mammals. Humans are one of approximately 5,400 mammal species that have so far been identified on Earth.

Several other unique characteristics can be used to distinguish mammals. Almost all mammals give birth to live young rather than laying eggs. Female mammals have special glands called mammaries, which produce milk to nourish their young. Mammals are also equipped with several different kinds of teeth. Most other vertebrate animals have just one kind of teeth or none. And those flaps of skin on the side of your head? Although we refer to them as ears, biologists call them

Mammals are a small group among the millions of species on Earth. They can be found almost everywhere on the planet and are adapted for life in many habitats—land, water, and air.

pinnae (the singular is *pinna*). Every vertebrate animal has ears, but only mammals have pinnae. They work like radar dishes, collecting sound and funneling it into the ear canal.

The most ancient and possibly the most unusual of the modern mammals are monotremes, such as the duck-billed platypus and echidna. Found on and around the continent of Australia, monotremes lay eggs rather than give birth. Many scientists believe that this links mammals to reptilian ancestors from 280 million years ago. Marsupials are a large group of mammals that live almost exclusively in Australia and South America. Newborn marsupials are tiny and underdeveloped. They crawl into the mother's belly pouch and attach to a mammary gland. A young marsupial may not emerge from the pouch for weeks, at which time it looks like a small version of the parent but still needs a lot of care. Most mammals fall into a group called placentals. These mammals give birth to live young. The placenta is a special organ that nourishes developing young inside the mother's womb. Humans are placental mammals, as are otters, horses, whales, and shrews. Placental mammals have adapted to live in almost every habitat on Earth. They walk on the land and swing in the highest trees, fly through the night, and swim in lakes and seas.

Carolus Linnaeus

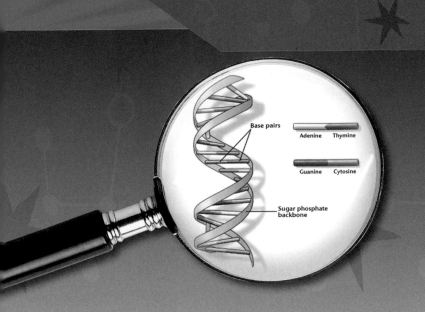

Base pairs

Adenine   Thymine

Guanine   Cytosine

Sugar phosphate
backbone

CLASSIFICATION

More than 2,400 years ago, the Greek philosopher Aristotle (384–322 BCE) began to think about how nature is organized. He imagined a ladder of life, with very simple plants and animals on the bottom rungs and more complex living things occupying the higher ones. Humans sat on the top rung of Aristotle's ladder. Swedish scientist Carolus Linnaeus (1707–1778 CE) was less concerned with deciding which organisms are most complex. He was curious about the relationships between species. Linnaeus devised a sophisticated classification system called taxonomy. This system required several steps. First he made a detailed list describing the organism's features. He might say that a deer has fur, four legs, hooves, and so forth. Organisms with similar characteristics were placed in groups. This approach sometimes led to mistakes. For example, Linnaeus initially mistook whales for fish—an error he later corrected. Taxonomy also includes a naming

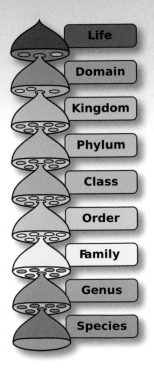

Life

Domain

Kingdom

Phylum

Class

Order

Family

Genus

Species

system. Each species has a two-part name. The first name, called a genus, reflects its membership in a group of related species. The second, or species, name is unique to each species in the genus.

Linnaeus's system has endured for 250 years. But one thing has changed: Modern scientists often rely more on genes than physical characteristics to classify species. Genes are found on DNA inside every cell. They provide unique instructions for building and operating each living thing. By examining genes, scientists can find patterns that are shared between related organisms. Genetics and traditional taxonomy have been used to classify the world's mammal species into 29 orders, or major groups.

Studying DNA may be the work of scientists, but anyone can classify. It's a useful way to learn more about mammals and to practice your observation skills.

MATERIALS

- a stack of magazines, or photos printed from the Internet
- scissors
- clear tape or a glue stick
- pencil and paper
- poster board

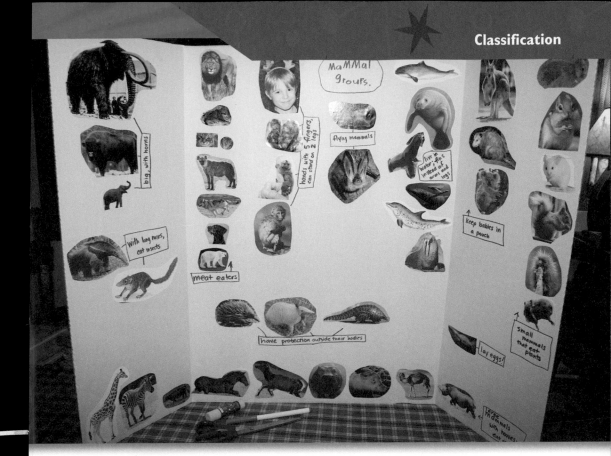

PROCEDURE

1. Find pictures of mammals in magazines or on the Internet. Try to be random in your selection (in other words, don't choose only one type of mammal). Cut them out.

2. Observe each picture individually. Make a table listing the features of each mammal that you think are important to its way of life.

3. When you have looked at all of the pictures, review the table. You may see some overlap, with mammals sharing one or more features. These are clues to help you form taxonomic groups. What if some mammals fit into several groups? Your job is to determine which feature(s) suggest the strongest relationship.

4. When you feel confident with your selection of groups, tape or glue the pictures to the poster board. Arrange the images by group. Next to each group, list the features you used to classify them.

5. How similar is your classification to the one used by biologists? Visit your local library to consult a book listing mammal orders, or use the Burke Museum's web page "Meet the Mammals." (The web address is provided at the end of this book.)

WATCHING WILDLIFE

Sit outside for a little while and several different kinds of wild birds are likely to fly past. But mammals are much harder to observe. Aside from squirrels and chipmunks, mammals are generally shy and prefer to avoid human company. Those that live near people may come out at dusk or dawn, or wait for total darkness. Other mammals are near, but wait to appear until the area seems clear of human activity. A wildlife blind can allow you to watch animals in their natural habitat, behaving as they do when people aren't around.

MATERIALS
- a large cloth (sheet, tablecloth, or bedspread) in dark earth tones such as brown or green
- scissors
- string
- pencil and paper
- binoculars

Wild mammals consider humans to be a threat. A wildlife blind provides camouflage, allowing you to blend into the environment. Sit behind it long enough and remain quiet; you may see rabbits, squirrels, or deer.

PROCEDURE

1. Ask a parent for permission to use a large cloth (sheet, tablecloth, or bedspread) for this project. Before you leave home, cut small holes near the four corners of the cloth. Use the scissors to make several narrow slits in different parts of the cloth as "windows." Also cut four pieces of string, each 24 inches long.

2. Search for a natural spot in your yard or neighborhood. Densely planted areas are good; these offer shelter and food for mammals.

3. Tie a length of string to each hole in the cloth.

4. Tie the other end of each string to a branch or other secure hold so that the cloth is stretched out with the bottom edge along the ground.

5. Camouflage your blind using some leaves and other materials from the local environment.

6. If possible, leave the blind in place for a few days. Mammals may check it out as a new object in their environment, but they will learn to ignore it. Then you can settle in behind it to watch and learn. Plan to spend a block of time behind your screen. Make sketches and notes about what you see. Notice the diversity of mammals you see, but also the numbers of each kind. What are their most common behaviors? Do they interact with each other? Think of new questions, and share your discoveries with friends and family.

The grizzly bear
is an extremely
heavy animal, but
its large feet
spread out its
weight so that it
doesn't sink very
deeply into mud.
If you find grizzly
tracks, **DO NOT**
follow them!

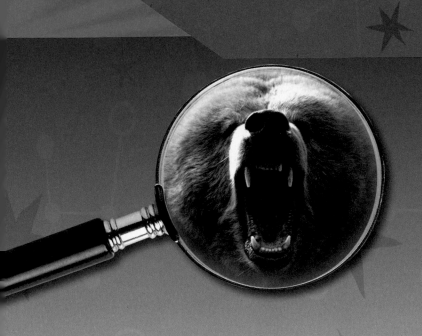

TRACKS

A different way to "observe" mammals is by tracking—looking for signs left by the animals as they passed by. Tracking is like solving a mystery in nature. You may find gnawed twigs along a path, or clumps of hair among the leaves. Male deer sometimes leave huge scrapes when they rub their antlers on the bark of trees. Scat provides another good clue that mammals have been around. Scat is their excrement, and it often contains bones, hair, and other undigested materials that reveal a mammal's diet. Another interesting and common piece of evidence is tracks. These may last for days in mud or snow. Each mammal species has a unique set of tracks, and with experience you can learn to identify them. Tracks also indicate what the individual animal was doing as it passed by. For example, tracks are spaced closely when a mammal walks; when it runs, they are far apart. Naturalists often make casts of these tracks as souvenirs or to teach others about animal behavior. Try this simple activity to preserve mammal tracks from your yard or a local park. You may need the assistance of a partner or adult.

MATERIALS
- cardboard
- scissors
- string
- 2 paper clips
- clean plastic storage container
- plastic spoon
- plaster of Paris mix
- water
- old toothbrush or cloth

PROCEDURE

1. Before you leave, cut some cardboard into two strips. Each should be 12 inches long and 1.5 inches wide. Also cut a few pieces of string in 2- or 3-inch lengths.

2. Collect your materials in a backpack or bag, and take them with you as you search for tracks. Tracks are often found along woodland paths and near water, but you may find some in your own backyard! Look for bare spots where the ground is soft.

3. When you find a good set of tracks, bend the cardboard into a ring and attach the ends together with a paperclip. If this ring is not large enough to encircle your tracks, attach both strips of cardboard into a single ring using two paperclips.

4. Pour plaster of Paris mix into the plastic storage container. The amount needed will depend on the size of your track and ring mold. The rule is to use two parts plaster of Paris to one part water. Mix the plaster until there are no dry lumps. It should have about the same consistency as pancake batter.

5. Tap the plastic container on the ground once to remove air bubbles, then carefully pour the plaster onto the ground inside your cardboard mold. It will fill the track and should cover the bottom of the mold.

6. Place the pieces of string atop the plaster. You can also add a few small twigs to make the cast sturdier. Allow the cast to harden in the air for half an hour, longer if necessary.

7. The finished cast should be cool and hard to the touch. At this point you can lift it up by gently wiggling the edges. Be patient if it seems

stuck. At home, allow the cast to set for a few more days. Then it can be cleaned with a damp toothbrush or cloth. Plaster casts can be painted, and will last for years unless they are dropped.

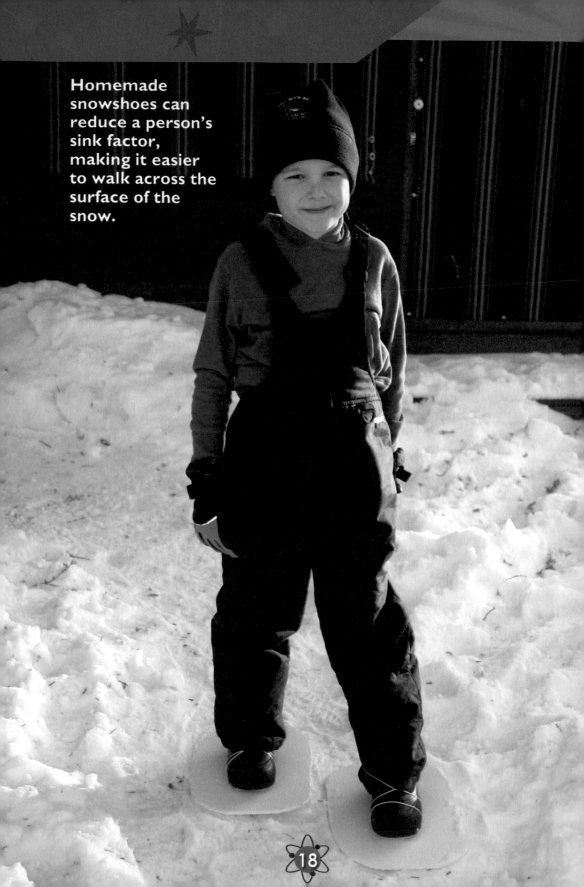

Homemade snowshoes can reduce a person's sink factor, making it easier to walk across the surface of the snow.

SHOWSHOES

Have you ever tried to walk through deep snow? Your feet sink in with every step, and you never know when you'll fall into a hidden hole. It's an exhausting way to travel, and can be dangerous. The problem is sink factor, a ratio of weight to foot area. For example, deer are large mammals. Although a deer's weight is distributed on four legs, its legs and hooves are so narrow that its sink factor is very high. Yet some mammals that live in snowy regions can run easily across the surface of the snow. What's their secret? Big feet! Large feet spread the weight of the body over a wider area. Rabbits have unusually long hind feet, while all four paws of lynxes are extra wide.

The rabbit's big feet inspired ancient humans in cold climates to build wide shoes for striding on snow. Native Americans used snowshoes, as did Viking people more than 1,200 years ago. You can make simple snowshoes and calculate the difference it makes in your sink factor.

MATERIALS

- poster board or heavy cardboard (such as from a large shipping box)
- boots
- pencil
- ruler
- scissors
- graph paper
- calculator
- heavy string
- scale

PROCEDURE

1. Lay the cardboard on a flat surface. Place your boot in the center and draw an outline of it.
2. Remove the boot. Draw a larger outline approximately 4 inches outside the original. Cut this out.
3. Repeat steps 1 and 2 for the other boot.
4. Place your boots back atop the cardboard. Make a mark on the cardboard beside where your laces tie. Do this on each side of both boots.
5. Measure a line two inches from these marks, toward the place where your toes will be. Mark these spots.
6. Use the edge of the scissors to carefully poke holes at these eight points.
7. Measure and cut lengths of string that are long enough to lace through the holes in the snowshoes and tie them onto your boots.
8. Find your sink factor without snowshoes. Weigh yourself on a household scale, obtaining the result in kilograms rather than pounds. Then trace the original outline of one boot onto graph paper. Count the number of squares occupied by your boot. Graph paper is usually drawn in square centimeters. Divide your weight in kilograms by the area of your boot in square centimeters.
9. Repeat step 8 using the area of your snowshoes. You may need to estimate for this figure, as the snowshoes will be larger than most graph paper. In this case measure the length of the snowshoe and its width (in centimeters); multiply to get the area. Alternatively, use two pieces of graph paper to trace the snowshoe and obtain your result. How does your sink factor change with the snowshoes?
10. On a snowy day, take a walk without your snowshoes. Then put them on and see if you can feel the difference. For best results, be sure to lift the front of your foot high with each step. Have fun!

Squirrels are master thieves when the treasure is birdseed.

BAFFLING!

You might enjoy watching dolphins because they are so energetic and clever. Big cats, such as tigers and lions, attract attention for their power and grace. Monkeys amuse and impress us with their antics, and apes always fascinate because they are like humans in so many ways. Animal behavior is a dynamic science. Each year researchers learn a great deal about the lives of mammals simply by watching them in action.

Squirrels are among the most common mammals in North America. You can observe them in cities, on farms, and in remote wilderness areas. A squirrel might seem uninteresting, but there's a reason these rodents are found everywhere. They are smart, persistent, and adapt to new situations quickly.

Has your family ever tried to keep a squirrel away from a bird feeder? It's not an easy task. In this activity, you will set up a baffle—a series of obstacles designed to keep squirrels away from a bird feeder. Observe the squirrels' behavior as they try to overcome the baffle. Will they win?

MATERIALS

- an adult
- 2 pieces of ³/₁₆-inch-thick foam board
- aluminum foil
- large cooking pot lid
- clothesline (cloth or plastic-coated)
- clothespins
- scissors
- pencil
- hanging bird feeder
- mixed bird seed (a variety with sunflower and/or peanuts will appeal most to squirrels)
- pliers (optional)

Homemade baffling

Dome-shaped
squirrel baffle

PROCEDURE

1. Lay the foam board on a flat surface. Use a pencil to trace the outline of a cooking pot lid on the board. Make 4 of these large circles and cut them out.
2. Cover the surface of each circle with aluminum foil.
3. Use the pencil to carefully poke a hole through the center of each circle. The hole should be just large enough to insert the clothesline.
4. With an adult, choose a place outside where you can hang the clothesline. It should be at least six feet above the ground to prevent squirrels from jumping up to reach it.
5. Tie one end of the clothesline in your chosen location. Make sure the knot is secure. (It may be helpful to pull it tight with pliers.)
6. Insert the clothesline through the holes of two circles, the hanger on the feeder, and then the other two circles. Tie the other end of the line.
7. Space the four circles 2 to 3 feet apart toward the center of the line. Clip a clothespin on each side of each circle to keep it from tipping.
8. Add some birdseed to the bird feeder.
9. Find a place from which to quietly watch. It may take a few hours for the squirrels to find your feeder, so check periodically. How long does a single squirrel try to overcome the baffle, and what methods does it use, before it gives up? Can you tell if more than one squirrel attempts to reach the food? Do any squirrels succeed? If so, what changes could you make to improve the baffle?

IN A PACK

Mammals can be grouped according to their eating habits as herbivores, carnivores, and omnivores. Herbivores eat only plants, while carnivores are meat eaters. Omnivores consume a diet containing a mix of plants and meat.

Aside from raising young, obtaining food takes up more time than any other activity in the life of a mammal. Each species solves this problem in a unique way. Pandas and koalas are herbivores that live alone. These mammals may spend hours in the same spot, plucking and chewing leaves. Caribou are also herbivores, but they live in huge herds that graze while moving across the northern tundra. The mountain lion is a solitary carnivore, while dolphins hunt in large groups.

Wolves also hunt in packs. By cooperating, wolves can kill prey much larger than themselves. A wolf pack is much more than a hunting team. It is a society with complex roles and rules. The pack has leaders and followers, who exhibit different behaviors. Confident or aggressive body posture suggests a leader. Obedient or fearful wolves are usually followers (though they may show more confidence around young pups). This status can be read in every part of a wolf's behavior, from its

tail position and facial expression to the order in which it eats after a kill.

Domestic dogs are the distant relatives of wild wolves, and they also show pack behavior. Most follow human leaders, but the rules can change when dogs get together. You may never see a wild wolf pack, but you can study pack behavior by watching dogs interact at a park.

PROCEDURE

1. Learn more about wolf behavior and social structure. Visit the International Wolf Center web site at http://www.wolf.org/wolves/learn/basic/biology/biology.asp, or find a book on wolves at your local library.
2. Identify behaviors that are typical of dominant and submissive wolves. Make charts listing each set of behaviors.
3. Make a prediction about the behaviors of domestic dogs. Will more dogs be dominant or submissive, or will they be equal?
4. Visit a setting that is popular with dog walkers. Find a place to sit and spend at least one hour just watching. If a dog exhibits a behavior that is on either of your lists, place a tally mark in the chart. Add only one tally per dog for each behavior.
5. At the end of your study period, total the tallies. Which behaviors were most common? Do the results support your prediction? Explain why or why not. If you plan to share your results, prepare bar graphs of the data.

A bat box

BUILD A BAT BOX

One-fifth of all mammal species in the world are bats. They are the only mammals that can fly, with arm and hand bones that have been adapted as wings. Most bat species eat insects, contributing to the control of pest insect populations such as beetles, moths, and mosquitoes. Nectar- and pollen-feeding bats play the same role at night as bees and hummingbirds do during the day: they pollinate a wide variety of night-blooming plants, from crop fruits to cacti. Bats that consume fruit spread seeds that help regenerate rain forests.

Bats need habitats in which to find these foods, but they also need places to roost (sleep, hibernate, and raise young). Many prefer caves. Others like to roost in trees. It can be difficult to find this habitat in urban areas, so bats may choose less desirable structures such as attics. A bat box is a much better option. You'll need an adult to help with construction.

The best time to put up a bat box is early spring, but you can add one to your neighborhood anytime. Just be patient; it may take bats a while to find it. Once they settle in, it will be fascinating to keep an eye on these wild neighbors, which otherwise are rarely seen.

MATERIALS

- untreated wood plank (6 inches wide by ¾ inch thick, sold in different lengths at hardware and lumber stores)
- handsaw or electric saw (to be used by **an adult**)
- pencil
- white carpenter's glue
- about 10 one-inch galvanized screws
- screwdriver (cordless optional)
- tarpaper and thumbtacks (optional)
- drill (optional; to be used by **an adult**)
- 2 or 3 three-inch nails
- hammer

NEVER DISTURB OR TOUCH BATS OR OTHER WILDLIFE

PROCEDURE

1. **Your adult helper** will need to saw the plank into several lengths.
   - a 10-inch-long backboard
   - a 6-inch-long frontboard
   - three wood strips, each 1 inch wide by 6 inches long

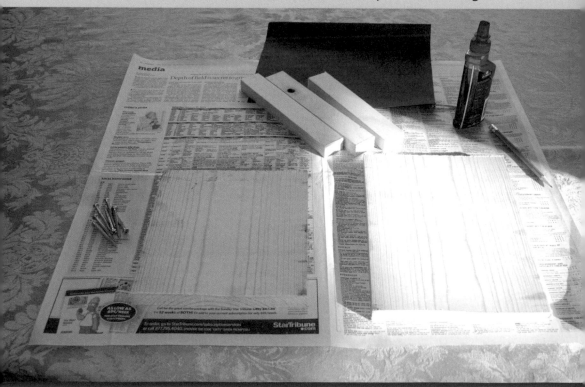

2. Lay the backboard on a flat work surface. Place the frontboard on top of the backboard, with one inch of space at the top. Trace around the frontboard with a pencil.

3. Remove the frontboard, and arrange the wood strips along the top and two sides of your traced line. The strips should rest on their narrow sides. Glue them in place with carpenter's glue so that the edges fit tightly together, forming a square with no bottom.

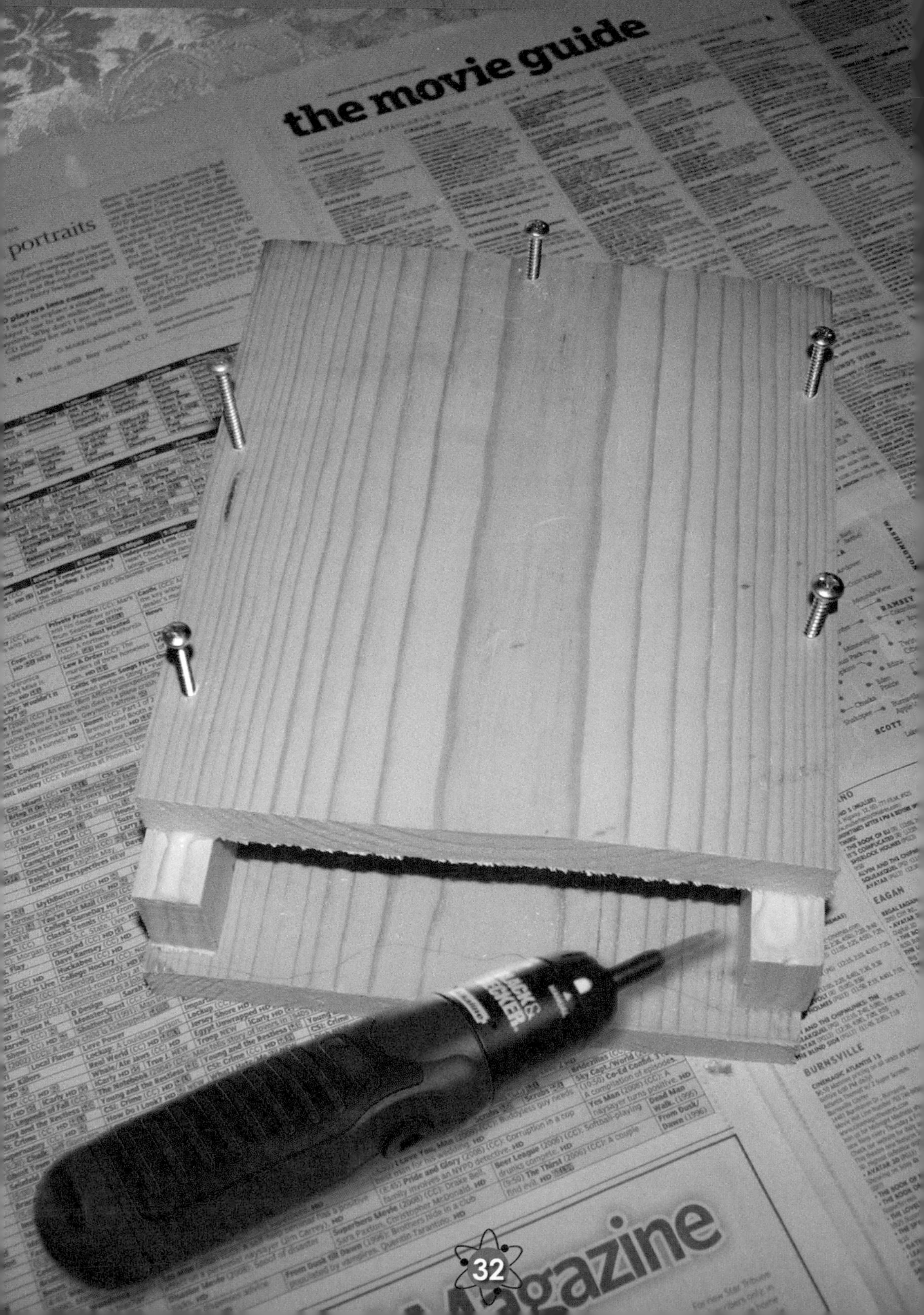
the movie guide
portraits

4. Apply glue to the top edges of the strips. Place the frontboard carefully atop them, aligning the edges. Use one-inch screws on each edge to affix the frontboard to the strips.
5. If available, tack a strip of tarpaper over the frontboard. This will cause the box to absorb heat, which appeals to bats.
6. **Have an adult** help you hang the box. If possible, drill a one-quarter-inch hole in the middle of the narrow section of board at the top of the box. Choose a spot that is 12 feet or higher above the ground, preferably facing south or southeast. It's better to mount your box on the wall of a building (but not your house) instead of using a tree; bats like a lot of sun rather than shade. Hammer a three-inch nail into the spot. To mount the box, slip the hole over the nail. Once the box is hung, you can add one or two nails just below the box to keep it from slipping.

A hollow tree provides the perfect nesting habitat for squirrels, offering space to store food and raise their young away from predators. When no hollows are available, squirrels build ball-shaped nests called dreys.

POPULATION CENSUS

Squirrels hop across suburban lawns every day. They raid bird feeders and scrabble like acrobats across telephone wires. But where do these creatures go with all that food, and how many live in your neighborhood? Scientists have several ways to answer questions like these. The most basic approach is observation. Go outside and watch a squirrel. Follow it as best you can for a period of time, and see what you find out.

Some of the results will depend on the species of squirrel being observed. By far the most common species in North America is the gray squirrel. The gray squirrel's body is usually about 10 inches long, with a fluffy tail that's slightly shorter than this. Despite the name, gray squirrels can also be coal black or occasionally white. Aside from color, a good way to separate this species from others is its lack of fur around the ears.

Gray squirrels will nest in the hollows of live trees when possible, but they often build nests from twigs and leaves. These basketball-sized dreys are hollow and may be lined with moss, fur, and dried grass for warmth and comfort. Dreys are usually positioned high in trees, at the fork of two branches. They are well concealed in summer, when trees are flush with leaves. Autumn and winter, when deciduous trees are bare, are the best times to look for squirrel dreys.

To learn the size of a population, a scientist will take a census. The simplest kind of census is called an actual count, in which the scientist records the number of individuals seen in a given area. In this activity, you will estimate the population of squirrels in a park or open space.

Eight squirrel nests (black circles) and two possible nests (red circles) adorn a deciduous tree.

MATERIALS
- paper and pencil
- binoculars
- calculator

PROCEDURE

1. Identify a study area. You'll need an area about the size of a square city block. (The average city block is about one-eighth of a mile, or about 650 feet, per side.) Ideally your chosen spot will have plenty of deciduous trees (those that lose their leaves in winter).

2. Locate a squirrel drey along one edge of your study area. Morning and evening are the best times to watch, as this is when squirrels are most active. Observe the drey for at least half an hour. Your goal is to determine how many squirrels use this nest. Record this number as the actual count of squirrels at this location. (If the nest shows no activity after two observations, try again at a different location.)

3. Repeat step 2 at a second active drey in your study area.

4. Add the total number of squirrels seen in both dreys. Divide by two. If your result is a fraction, round to the nearest whole number. This number is called an average. It suggests the typical number of squirrels in each drey in your study area. (Averages are more accurate when calculated from larger sample sizes. Observe a few more dreys if you have time, and divide by the number of dreys when calculating your average.)

5. Walk through your entire study area, counting every drey you see.

6. Multiply the number of dreys you observed by the average number of squirrels per drey. The result is a population estimate. You did not actually see this many squirrels, but it is a reasonable guess. How might scientists use population estimates when studying squirrels and other mammals?

BONES

It's no wonder that early scientists found it hard to classify mammals. Who would guess that humans, bats, and whales are related? Bats fly like birds and whales are huge oceanic swimmers. Bats are furry, while humans have just a little hair, and whales appear to have none at all. It takes close examination to find the similarities between such dissimilar groups of mammals. Some of the proof lies deep within their bodies. The skeleton is a good place to begin such comparisons.

MATERIALS
- Images of human, bat, whale, and bird skeletons (found on the Internet)
- colored highlighters or markers

PROCEDURE
1. Use the Internet to find images of human, bat, whale, and bird skeletons. (Simple image searches such as "whale skeleton" should return good results on most web browsers.) Birds and mammals are

both members of the vertebrate group of animals, which have backbones.

2. Print out the four images and lay them side by side on a table.

3. Select a highlighter and outline the human spine. Find the same bones on the bat, whale, and bird skeletons. Use the same color to highlight the spine, skull, and ribs on all the images.

4. Use a different color to highlight the arm and hand bones on your images. Which animals have similar hands and arms? Which animal is different? Can you guess why?

5. Use a third highlighter to outline the bones of each animal's legs and feet. Now where do you see similarities? How can you explain differences? If you did not know that these were birds and mammals, would you have been able to use the bones of these animals to place them into groups?

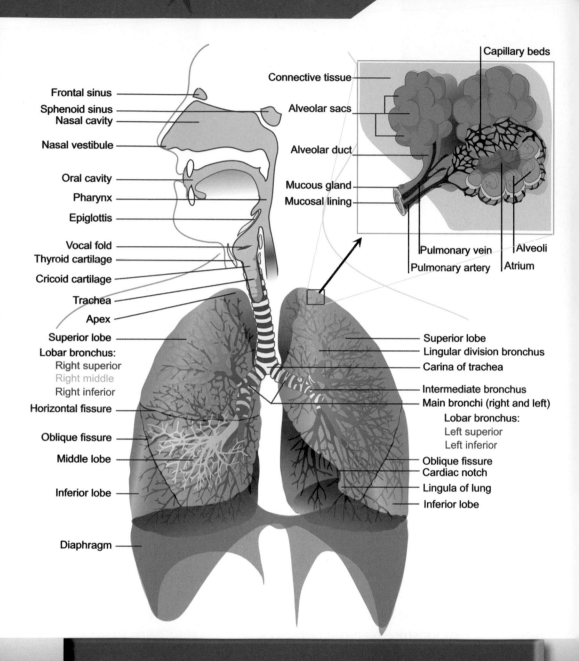

Capillary beds

Connective tissue

Alveolar sacs

Frontal sinus

Sphenoid sinus
Nasal cavity

Nasal vestibule

Alveolar duct

Oral cavity

Pharynx

Mucous gland
Mucosal lining

Epiglottis

Vocal fold

Thyroid cartilage

Cricoid cartilage

Pulmonary vein
Pulmonary artery

Alveoli
Atrium

Trachea

Apex

Superior lobe

Lobar bronchus:
  Right superior
  Right middle
  Right inferior

Horizontal fissure

Oblique fissure

Middle lobe

Inferior lobe

Diaphragm

Superior lobe
Lingular division bronchus
Carina of trachea

Intermediate bronchus
Main bronchi (right and left)
Lobar bronchus:
  Left superior
  Left inferior
Oblique fissure
Cardiac notch
Lingula of lung
Inferior lobe

The human respiratory system is large and complex. Its role is to carry oxygen into the body and remove wastes. A person's respiratory rate changes with exercise, bringing in more oxygen to help the muscles work.

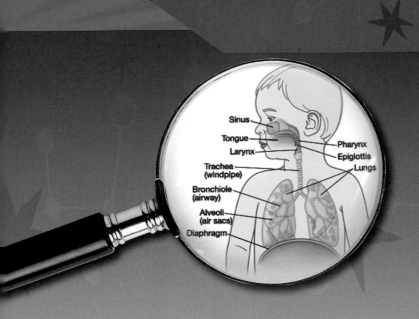

Sinus
Tongue
Larynx
Trachea (windpipe)
Bronchiole (airway)
Alveoli (air sacs)
Diaphragm
Pharynx
Epiglottis
Lungs

RESPIRATION

Humans sometimes feel separate from nature, but they share all the characteristics common to mammals. Among these is the diaphragm. It's a wide, dome-shaped band of muscle that separates the body cavity into two halves. Your lungs and heart are located above the diaphragm, while the organs of digestion, excretion, and reproduction lie below it. When the diaphragm expands downward, the upper section of your body cavity grows larger. Air is pulled into your lungs to fill the space, and tiny pockets in the soft tissue of the lungs expand like balloons. This is called inhalation. (You can take a breath on purpose, but your brain usually controls this process.) Oxygen from the lungs is carried through the bloodstream to the heart and body. It returns in a loop to the lungs. When the diaphragm relaxes, you exhale, and air is forced out of the lungs. Exhalation releases waste products such as carbon dioxide.

The process of breathing is called respiration, and the organs involved make up the respiratory system. The number of respirations per minute, or respiratory rate, varies among mammal species. Age and health status can also have an impact. For adults, a healthy respiratory

MATERIALS
- a partner
- chair
- stopwatch
- pencil
- plain paper
- graph paper

rate is 15 to 20 breaths per minute. Results for school-aged children and teenagers may be slightly higher.

Respiratory rate changes rapidly with exercise. In fact, increasing the rate of respiration is one of the goals of exercise. More oxygen moves into the bloodstream, causing the heart to pump faster. This provides much-needed oxygen to hardworking muscles, which use it to make energy and keep working. You can test the effect of exercise on respiration in this simple experiment.

PROCEDURE

1. Sit in a chair with your feet on the floor. Have your partner use a stopwatch to measure your respiration rate for exactly one minute. This is your resting rate. Write the data on a plain sheet of paper.
2. Spend exactly one minute running in place. When finished, immediately have your partner measure your respiration rate, using the same procedures as in step 1.
3. Wait 15 minutes, allowing your respiration to slow down to the resting rate.
4. Time yourself again, this time for 10 minutes of vigorous, nonstop activity. Run in place again, ride a bike, jump rope, or do any activity of your choice. When the time is up, have your partner measure your respiration rate as in step 1.
5. Use graph paper to show your results. A bar graph is useful for this kind of data. Mark the *x*-axis with three labels: resting rate, 1 minute, and 10 minutes. The *y*-axis should be labeled with respiratory rates. Make sure that you divide the chart into even intervals (by 5 or 10, for example) for accuracy. Draw a bar representing the respiratory rate for each test. Does exercise change the rate of respiration? What is the effect of a longer period of exercise?
6. You can extend this activity by comparing your results to those of your partner and family members.

Books

Beer, Amy-Jane, and Pat Morris. *Mammals.* Redding, CT: Brown Bear
    Books, 2006.

Burton, John (ed.). *Mammals of the United States and Canada.* Chicago, IL:
    World Book, 2007.

Phelps, Earl R. *How to Draw Magnificent Mammals.* Cleveland, OH: Phelps
    Publications, 2006.

Pobst, Sandra. *Animals on the Edge: Science Races to Save Species
    Threatened With Extinction.* Washington, D.C.: National Geographic,
    2008.

Steffof, Rebecca. *Sea Mammals.* Tarrytown, NY: Marshall Cavendish
    Benchmark, 2009.

Walker, Richard. *Nature Ranger.* New York: DK Publishing, 2006.

Works Consulted

Attenborough, David. *The Life of Mammals.* Princeton, NJ: Princeton
    University Press, 2002.

Benyus, Janine M. *The Field Guide to Wildlife Habitats of the Western United
    States.* New York: Fireside, 1989.

Clutton-Brock, Juliet. *A Natural History of Domesticated Mammals.*
    Cambridge, UK: Cambridge University Press, 1999.

Muir, Hazel. "Ancient Remains Could Be Oldest Pet Cat." *New Scientist,*
    April 8, 2004. Retrieved October 17, 2009. http://www.newscientist.
    com/article/dn4867-ancient-remains-could-be-oldest-pet-cat.html

Murie, Olaus J. *A Field Guide to Animal Tracks.* Boston: Houghton Mifflin
    Company, 1974.

New York State Department of Health. "Assessment Tools." Retrieved
    November 2, 2009. http://www.health.state.ny.us/nysdoh/ems/pdf/
    assmttools.pdf

Nowak, Ronald M. *Walker's Bats of the World.* Baltimore, MD: The Johns
    Hopkins University Press, 1994.

Wilson, D. E., & D.M. Reeder (Eds.). *Mammal Species of the World: A
    Taxonomic and Geographic Reference.* Baltimore, MD: Johns Hopkins
    University Press.

On the Internet

American Museum of Natural History: Biodiversity: Everything Counts
  http://www.amnh.org/ology/index.php?channel=biodiversity
Bat Conservation International
  http://www.batcon.org
BBC: All Mammals
  http://www.bbc.co.uk/nature/class/Mammal/by/rank/all
Burke Museum of Natural History and Culture: Meet the Mammals
  http://www.washington.edu/burkemuseum/collections/
  mammalogy/mtm.php
Canadian Museum of Nature: Natural History Notebooks: Mammals
  http://nature.ca/Notebooks/english/mammpg.htm
National Geographic: Mammals
  http://animals.nationalgeographic.com/animals/mammals.html
National Zoo: North American Animals
  http://nationalzoo.si.edu/Animals/NorthAmerica/
  ForKids/default.cfm
Smithsonian Institution: North American Mammals
  http://www.mnh.si.edu/mna/

adaptation (aa-dap-TAY-shun)—Any physical feature or behavior that suits a living thing for its lifestyle.

biodiversity (by-oh-dih-VER-sih-tee)—The total variety of life in an area.

carnivore (KAR-nih-vor)—An animal that eats other animals.

cast—A mold made in the tracks of an animal.

census (SEN-sus)—A scientific study to determine the size of an animal population.

classification (klas-ih-fih-KAY-shun)—A system used to place related things into groups.

drey (DRAY)—A leaf nest built by squirrels.

gene (JEEN)—One of the segments of DNA located in cells, which provide unique instructions for building and operating each living thing.

herbivore (ER-buh-vor)—An animal that eats plants.

invertebrate (in-VER-tuh-brut)—An animal without a backbone.

mammary (MAA-muh-ree)—A gland, found only in mammals, that produces milk to feed the young.

marsupial (mar-SOO-pee-ul)—A type of mammal that gives birth to tiny young that complete their development in the mother's pouch.

monotreme (MAH-noh-treem)—A type of mammal that lays eggs rather than giving birth to live young.

omnivore (OM-nih-vor)—An animal that eats a mixed diet of plants and meat.

placenta (pluh-SEN-tuh)—An organ that nourishes developing young inside the mother's womb.

roost—A resting place for bats or birds.

sink factor—A ratio of weight to foot area that describes an animal's risk of sinking into snow, sand, or other soft substances.

species (SPEE-sheez)—A group of living things that are like each other but unique from other living things.

taxonomy (tak-SAH-nuh-mee)—A system used by scientists to classify and name living things.

vertebrate (VER-teh-brut)—Any animal with a spinal cord.

adaptation 5

animal behavior 23

antlers 15

apes 23

Aristotle 7

baffles 22, 23–25

bat boxes 28, 29–33

bats 28, 29–33, 38–39

bears 14

biodiversity 4

bird feeders 23–25

birds 4, 11, 28, 38–39

bones 4, 15, 29, 38

carbon dioxide 41

caribou 26

carnivores 26

cast (tracks) 15–17

cats (big) 23

chipmunks 11

classification 7–9, 38

deciduous trees 36

deer 15, 19

diaphragm 41

DNA 8

dogs (domestic) 27

dolphins 23, 26

dreys 34, 35–37

ears (see also *pinnae*) 4

echidnas 5

fish 4, 7

genes 8

genetics 8

genus 8

heart 41

herbivores 26

horses 5

invertebrates 4

koalas 26

Linnaeus, Carolus 6, 7–8

lions (African) 23

lungs 41

lynx 19

mammary glands 4–5

marsupials 5

monkeys 23

monotremes 5

mountain lions 26

Native Americans 19

omnivores 26

otters 5

pandas 26

pinnae 5

placental mammals 5

platypus 5

pollination 29

population census 35–37

rabbits 19

respiratory system 40, 41–43

roost 29

scat 15

shrews 5

sink factor 19–21

skeletal system 38–39

snowshoes 18, 19–21

species 4, 7–8, 15, 26, 29, 35, 41

squirrels 11, 22, 23–25, 34, 35–37

taxonomy 7

teeth 4

tigers 23

tracking 14, 15–16

vertebrates 4, 39

Vikings 19

whales 5, 7, 38–39

wildlife blind 11–13

wolves 26–27

ABOUT THE AUTHOR

Christine Petersen is a freelance writer and environmental educator who lives near Minneapolis, Minnesota. A former field biologist who researched bats, Petersen also taught middle school science. She has written more than thirty books for young people that cover a wide range of topics in social studies and science. When she's not writing, she conducts naturalist programs on bats and watches wildlife in her backyard.